Exploring the Solar System

Dakota Block

ROSEN
COMMON CORE
READERS

New York

Published in 2013 by The Rosen Publishing Group, Inc.
29 East 21st Street, New York, NY 10010

Book Design: Michael Harmon

Photo Credits: Cover Christos Georghiou/Shutterstock.com; p. 4 iStockphoto/Thinkstock.com; p. 5 John T. Takai/Shutterstock.com; p. 6 James Thew/Shutterstock.com; pp. 7, 8 vecotmart/Shutterstock.com; pp. 9, 10 Hemera/Thinkstock.com; p. 11 (asteroid belt) Gunnar Assmy/Shutterstock.com; p. 11 (asteroid) Mopic/Shutterstock.com; p. 12 Adastra/Taxi/Getty Images; pp. 13, 16 Luis Stortini Sabor aka CVADRAT/Shutterstock.com; p. 14 https://secure.flickr.com/photos/gsfc/6760135001/sizes/o/in/photostream/; p. 15 Dr_Flash/ Shutterstock.com; p. 17 Enrico Agostoni/Shutterstock.com; p. 18 SSSCC/Shutterstock.com; p. 19 MichaelTaylor/Shutterstock.com; p. 20 Digital Vision./Digital Vision/Getty Images; p. 21 Mike Brinson/The Image Bank/Getty Images.

Library of Congress Cataloging-in-Publication Data

Block, Dakota.
Exploring the solar system / Dakota Block.
p. cm. — (Exploring Earth and space)
Includes index.
ISBN: 978-1-4488-8857-3
6-pack ISBN: 978-1-4488-8858-0
ISBN: 978-1-4488-8572-5 (library binding)
1. Solar system—Juvenile literature. 2. Outer space—Exploration—Juvenile literature. I. Title.
QB501.3.B59 2013
523.2—dc23

2012012427

Manufactured in the United States of America

CPSIA Compliance Information: Batch #WS12RC: For further information contact Rosen Publishing, New York, New York at 1-800-237-9932.

Word Count: 554

Contents

A Space Community

Our solar system is like a big **community** in space. It's made up of the sun and the many space objects that move around it. Earth is part of the solar system.

Earth is a planet. Planets are large bodies in our solar system that move around the sun. Each planet has its own path around the sun. This path is called its orbit.

The sun is a star. It's made of different gases. These gases are very hot. The sun is much larger than the planets that move around it.

The planets closest to the sun are called the inner planets. There are four inner planets. They are Mercury, Venus, Earth, and Mars. They're made of rock.

The outer planets are the farthest from the sun. They're larger than the inner planets and are made of gas. The outer planets are Jupiter, Saturn, Uranus, and Neptune.

Most of the planets have small bodies that orbit them. These are called moons. Earth has one moon that you can see in the sky.

Some space objects that orbit the sun are too small to be called planets. They are known as **dwarf** planets. Pluto is one of these.

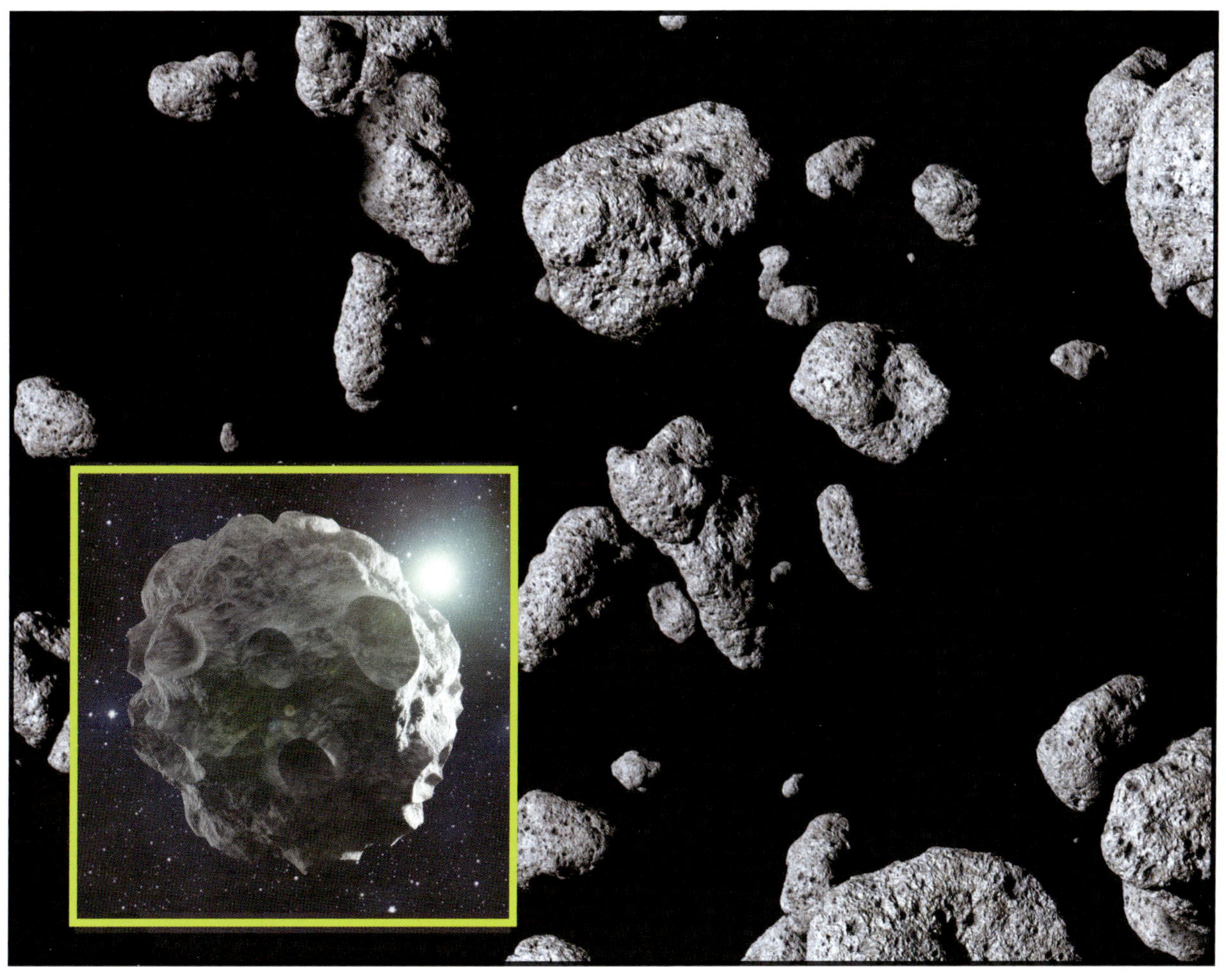

Asteroids (AS-tuh-royds) are large pieces of rock that also orbit the sun. Many asteroids follow the same orbit in a part of the solar system called the asteroid belt. It's between the inner and outer planets.

The Inner Planets

Mercury is the planet that's closest to the sun. It travels around the sun quickly. It makes one orbit in just 88 days. Earth takes a whole year to make one orbit!

Venus is a very hot planet. It's too hot for things to live there. Venus has many openings in the ground called volcanoes (vohl-KAY-nohs). Hot gases and **melted** rock come out of these volcanoes.

We live on planet Earth. It's the third planet from the sun. Earth is the only planet where we know things can live. There's a lot of water on Earth. Animals, plants, and people need water to live.

The fourth planet from the sun is Mars. It's called the Red Planet because its **soil** is red. This soil gets blown around during big storms on the planet. Mars is also a cold planet. Ice has been found there.

The Outer Planets

The outer planets are sometimes called gas giants. Jupiter is the first gas giant after the asteroid belt. It's the largest planet in our solar system.

There's a huge storm on Jupiter that has been going on for over 300 years. This storm can be seen from space! It's called the Great Red Spot.

Next to Jupiter, Saturn is the largest planet in the solar system. It's known for the many rings that go around it. These rings are made of ice. Saturn also has many moons.

The seventh planet in our solar system is Uranus.

It's made of gases that give it a blue-green color.

Uranus has rings, too. It has 11 rings.

The last planet is Neptune. It's the farthest planet from the sun and has the longest orbit. Neptune is made of gases like the other outer planets. These gases make the planet look bright blue.

Time to Explore!

It's fun to **explore** our solar system! There are many great things to discover about space. Would you like to be a space explorer when you grow up?

Our Solar System

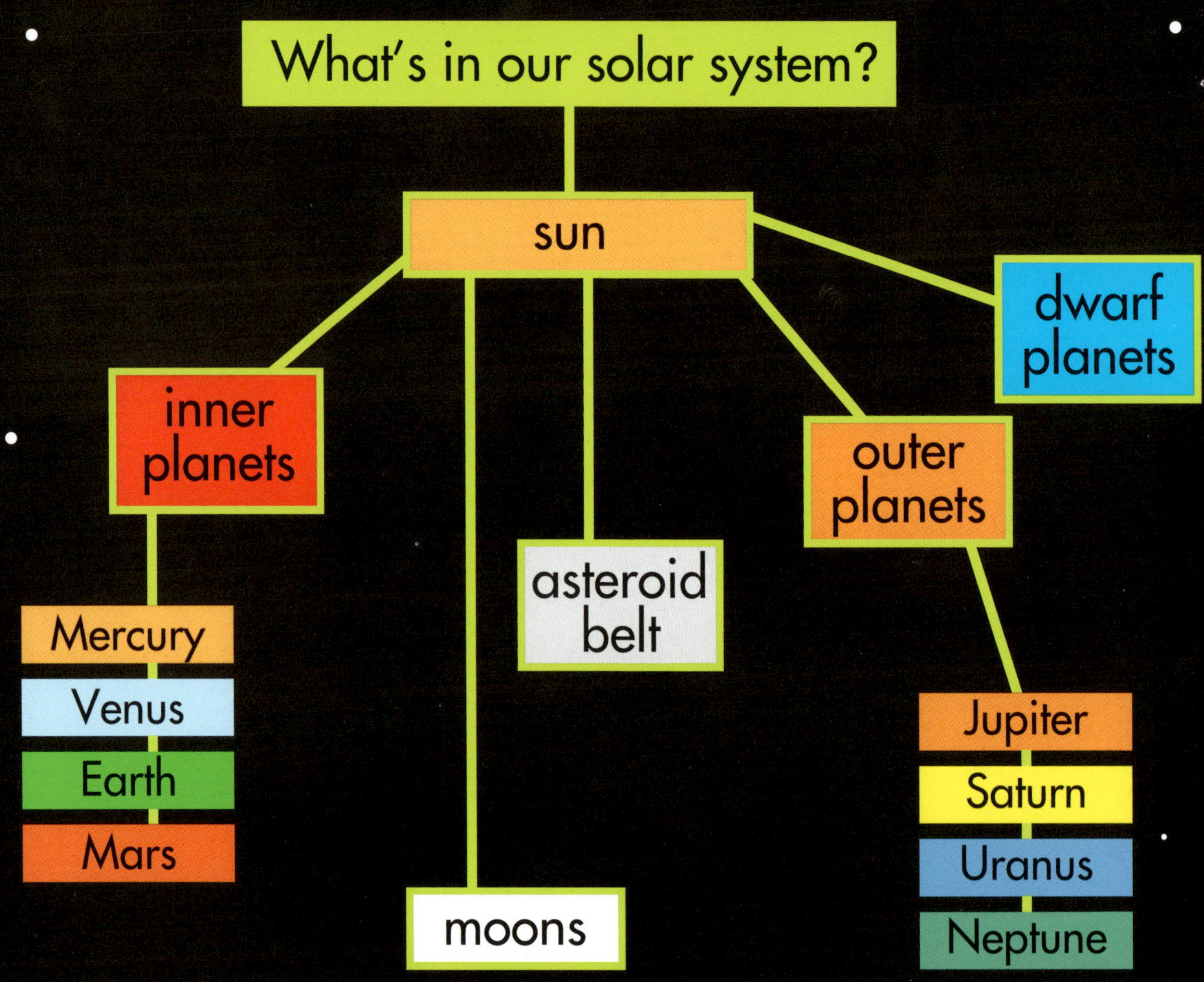

Glossary

community (kuh-MYOO-nuh-tee) A group of things that are close together.

dwarf (DWORF) Something that is much smaller than others of its kind.

explore (ihk-SPLOHR) To search something to find out more about it.

melted (MEHL-tuhd) Made soft and flowing because of heat.

soil (SOYL) Dirt.

Index

Due to the changing nature of Internet links, The Rosen Publishing Group, Inc., has developed an online list of websites related to the subject of this book. This site is updated regularly. Please use this link to access the list: **www.powerkidslinks.com/ees/solr**